Plucking Daisies

Alexandria Kennamer

BookLeaf Publishing

India | USA | UK

Presentation by *BookLeaf Publishing*

Web: www.bookleafpub.com

E-mail: info@bookleafpub.com

ISBN: 9789357215114

First edition 2023

*To every human who ever felt like they weren't
enough. And every human who ever felt they
were too much. Also, to the ones in between.
The world needs your love the most.*

ACKNOWLEDGEMENT

This endeavor would not have been possible without the support of my readers, Bookleaf Publishing, and my soul family. Thank you for believing in me. And a special thanks, to the ones who planted seeds of love and compassion in my heart along the way.

PREFACE

The pen is a dagger in her palms. It cuts through her most secret parts, splattering onto the pages in elegant, sprawling ink. Her soul bleeds into each sentence, yearning to be understood. "This is who I am." She whispers, behind the voice of another. "Here is the woman I keep buried inside."

-Transference

Wanderlust

As a child, I often played with imaginary things.
My sticks, were swords and wands.
The canopy of trees I lay under were an
undiscovered, magical land, lovingly calling me
home.
I held onto insignificant, slightly things.
The pebble in my pocket, a Dragon Egg,
awaiting countless millennia to hatch.
The duck feather I lifted tenderly from the
ground, a trinket to please the auspicious Fairy
Queen.

I spent many hours lost in a fantastical realm,
anointing Knights of Squirrels and brewing love
potions in my bucket cauldron with leaves,
petals and rainwater.
Oh, what a time that was! To be young, creative
and fearless.
Take me back to that little girl, the one who
slayed giants and held feasts for the Roly Polys.
Let me get lost once more in an Enchanted
Forest.
For this was the start of my Wanderlust.

Untethered

Before I met you,

I had to scream to be heard.

There was a time, when expectations were
swords, twisted hilt-deep into my chest.

Gaping, oozing wounds onto my soul-

and I had no right to be upset.

Before I met you,

I spent many nights alone.

Curled under the weight of the world,
crumbling,

wondering...

If my heart would ever find a home.

Oh, there were Fosters, no doubt.

Users,

Abusers,

Cheaters to boot.

They swooped in like vultures, under the
disguise of a mouse.

Fraying,

breaking,

disentangling all too soon.

And then your fingers

traced all of my scars and blemishes

with such tenderness

 - I trembled.

Where others found fault,

you saw

a warrior.

"Bold, brave, beautiful."

you whisper,

so sweetly, so simple.

The Tower

The Door hangs in its crevice.

A looming remnant of the life stripped from its bark.

There's a candle flickering in the window -burning out of light.

A little girl is broken, screaming from inside.

Rain beats upon the windows, rattling the pains,

Twisting, gnashing, gnarling, she cries.

Help me,

Light, bright, blinding, beautiful.

Hope.

She screams, thrashing, clashing-

ripping away from the anguish anchoring her
down.

Climbing out of the remnants,

She looks at the horizon, eyes brimming with
tears.

A warm breeze playfully tickles her face.

With each quivering step, everything falls into
place.

Home.

Angel Kisses

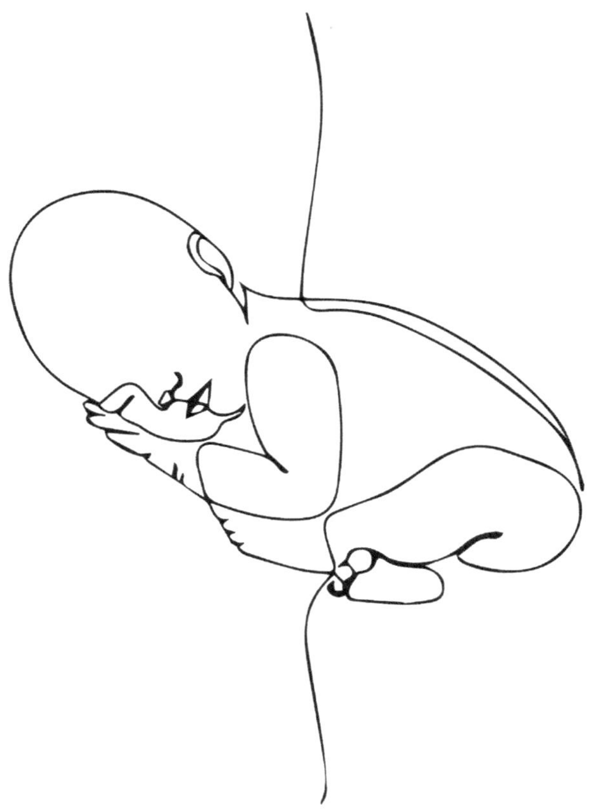

Sometimes, when the heavens open wide, and
thunder breaks the sky-
as lightning clashes and rain pours down,
I swear I feel you by my side.

As tears collect like dewdrops on a crisp, Spring
morning,
My heart sputters to a painful halt - stumbling,
crumbling as Winter closes in without warning.

But then, as dawn rises slowly on the horizon,
and the colors of your memory splay softly
amidst the morning sun-
I am warmed by your Angel Kisses for another
day has begun.

Fine China

Kintsugi is the Japanese art of putting broken pieces of pottery back together with gold. Thus, making a stronger, and more valuable item than what was damaged.

I came into this world frail and brand new. Through time, the coarse hands of life chipped and cracked me until I shattered. Dismayed, I tried to piece myself back together. I deceived myself by trying to deceive others into thinking I was still whole. One day, I accepted that I was broken and would never be the same. Liquid love, molten and oozing from my core, tacked the shards together into something fierce and beautiful to behold.

One of a kind, I was meant for more than to sit on display in a dusty curio cabinet. I took the fall, and out of the crumbles arose a masterpiece.

I am not sorry.

Masquerade

Love doesn't seek to destroy.
Love doesn't lie or manipulate.
Love doesn't leave you with an empty pit in
your stomach, desperately clawing at yourself to
find warmth.
Love doesn't envy what others have.
Love doesn't take and take and take.
Love doesn't spit in your face, just to turn
around and beg for pardon.
Love doesn't rip the scabs off unhealed wounds.
Love doesn't scream to be heard.
Love doesn't break your heart, on purpose.

Hate does.

Bloom

Sometimes, you do not grow where you are planted.

Maybe there's not enough sunlight.
Maybe the soil doesn't have enough nutrients.
Maybe there are larger plants prospering around
you while your leaves shrivel and your roots
ache.
Maybe the environment is not sustainable, no
matter how much you receive, the care just isn't
enough.
Whatever the reason, sometimes you must be
uprooted from the soil and replanted in a new
spot. A better spot.
But first, you must understand what is inhibiting
your growth.

Only then will you be able to bloom.

River of Life

My mouth is parched, my arms are weary.

I lift a shaky canister to cracked lips.

Just a sip. Just the tip of my tongue.

My well is empty.

"Lord, are you there?"

"Child, come to me."

I hear your whispers, soft and sweet.

You blow a gentle breeze against my sweltering
flesh.

A brief reprieve.

"Where are you?"

"Child, I'm here. Please see me."

The dunes around me are shifting.

My nostrils are burning from the sand.

I clench a tattered cloth to my face.

"God, do you hate me? Why won't you help me?"

"Child, I love you. My arms are open. I have sanctuary."

I fall to my knees in despair.

"I can't do this alone.

Please hear my prayers. Don't let me die out here!"

Out of the turmoil, a cup appears.

An angel opens their wings.

"Look up, Child. God has heard your prayers."

I stare in disbelief. For the cup holds less than a drop.

The Angel laughs.

"I know what you are thinking. Drink up."

O God, do you mock me?

"Child, one drink from this cup and your canister will be full for eternity."

With trembling hands, I take the goblet into my palms.

The drop slides onto my tongue.

I look up and the angel is gone.

The sands shift and a path begins to form.

With renewed energy I break into a run.

Oh, what a beautiful sight!

My spirit sings. My soul is alive.

With childlike wonder I plunge into the River of Life!

Seeing Ghosts

Let's stay here a moment,

swaying gently with the tall weeds,

a symphony of cicadas

humming around us.

A moment,

where we're still young

and basked in moonlight

as the stars whisper

our destiny from above:

A destiny we need not think about yet.

All too often,

I find myself tumbling

headfirst into the riverbanks

while you drift lazily

on by and wink.

Oh, how easy it is to melt into the past!

To live in a time

where your heart still beats with mine.

Philanthropy

Why do we have money for Mars?

When there are children

with swollen bellies

trying to silence their hunger

with mud from yards?

Why do we recycle?

If it wastes more than it saves?

Biodegradable is an option

available to help our Earth today.

Why do we hurt each other?

When we know what it's like

to live with aches.

Life isn't a competition

or compilation

of mistakes -

It's an opportunity

to love another,

each and every way.

Deliverance

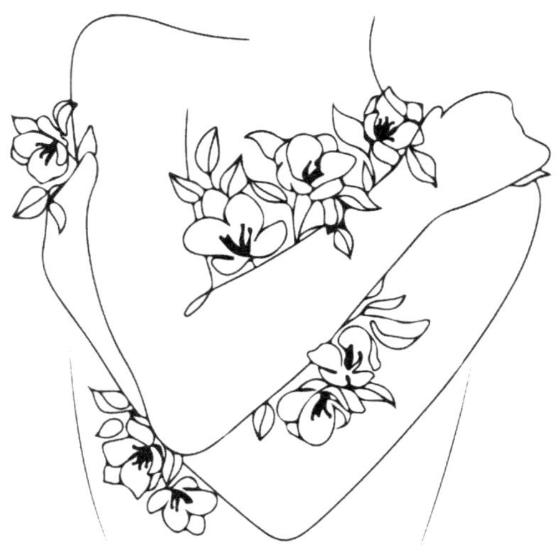

Every tear you shed while you cursed my name.

Every time I reached out to heal your pain.

Every prayer, every thought that crossed your
heart.

Every night you spent curled alone in the dark.

Every whisper and scream, Darling, I felt it.

Every time your heart broke, your hand-I held it.

You learned to be strong when you wanted to break.

You learned to be humble no matter the stakes.

You learned to be kind when others were cruel.

You learned to be bold and make your own rules.

Forged through fire into a weapon of steel.

I love you, Daughter, it's time to Heal

As Above, So Below

I am a tree.

My roots sink into soils that have hosted centuries of lives.

I am a honeybee.

Saving the world, one flower at a time.

I am a storm cloud passing by.

Bringing refreshment to the parched fields below.

I am a daisy.

Drink me as a tea, for many remedies.

I am a constellation in the sky.

Guiding countless lost travelers home.

I am a window cat.

Purring softly in the sun and flicking its tail.

I am a sign.

Come here to tell you that all is well.

I am a sea turtle.

Trusting the sands to guide my children into the
lapping arms of the ocean.

I am a person.

Kindly reaching out, to offer you a hand.

I am a wind-chime.

Singing softly, as I twirl along to my own
special dance.

My friend, Trauma

You come to me like an old friend.

And I have no fight

left in me

to send you with the wind.

So I embrace you,

With love and all my might.

In hopes that you will understand,

I did what I had to, in order to survive.

And there are nights

when the despair is too much.

Another piece of me peeled away

at your intolerable touch.

Then, I remember

the strength I gained.

And suddenly, it doesn't seem so bad

to live with you anymore.

Or the consequences

of being mad.

I can handle what happened,

as long as they're alright.

Me and my friend, Trauma,

waltz long into the night.

Addiction

One kiss is not enough,

To ease the burning for your touch.

Our love,

Is a castle in the sky.

Towering above a cloud of passion and lies.

29

Why do we deny

Ourselves the truth?

Glass hearts rattling through gaping wounds.

Ignoring the doom

that is to come,

Into your arms, again, I run.

Photosynthesis

I am a rose.

Soft

and tender,

yet my thorns

do provoke.

Pricking fingers

to warn

offenders away.

Though there is water

in my vase,

It is not

what I need

to be

sustained.

Starving for Attention

Some people throw you scraps
Just to satiate you.
And so, shortly after

You return to the table
Only to be chided for wanting more.
You are not a beggar,

Be careful who you dine with.

The Last Adventure

It was on my journey with Agony, that I stumbled into Gratitude. I asked her, where she found the strength to smile, when Shame had been hunting us for countless miles. She led us to a creek, where Endurance and Patience were wading in its banks.

I shook their hands, and they introduced me to their dear friend, Faith, who danced fondly with Grace. Grace, not to be mistaken for their sibling, Mercy- helped me learn to embrace Pain. For Pain, remains the greatest teacher of all, followed closely by Mistakes.

Somewhere along the way, I was visited by Death. Compassion tended to my wounds as Love held me to their chest. It was Love, that loaned me Courage to cast out Fear. And from Love, birthed Hope, as the end of our adventure together became clear.

Ikigai

I hope you find the courage

to hold your head high -

Even when the odds are stacked against

you.

When life is unfair, or people cruel

and nothing

seems to go your way

My wish, for you

is to take a break, reflect

And learn to appreciate the gray.

You are beautiful

I see the way you smile, kindly

Even when everything whole inside -

wants to explode.

In your life,

You will face many battles.

Know when to surrender

know when to fight.

And remember, a brilliant new day

dawns from every dark night.

Clipped Wings

You see a starving artist.

I see a bird.

Whose wings were clipped,

before it ever got the chance to soar.

Breaking the Cycle

There was a toothbrush

That I shared

Whenever I was forced to scrub

My tears off the floor

Nursing bruises and picking up

A drunken mess that was all yours

Now I stand with painted toes

In a joyous home

That has never known

Fits of violence

Or unnecessary woe

And you will never hurt me again

Sol

You are a star

beaming rays into the dark.

Betwixt the inky galaxies.

From there,

that place where

your soul cries for understanding

and warmth, and love to share.

Where kindness is radiating;

And forgiveness isn't scarce.

Your heart, my Darling,

Is where this loveliness resides.

You are the Sun, and my, how you shine!